Learn **French** with

Max et Mathilde

Les Jours de la Semaine
Days of the Week

A catalogue record for this book is available from the British Library

Published by Ladybird Books Ltd
80 Strand, London, WC2R 0RL
A Penguin Company

2 4 6 8 10 9 7 5 3 1

Image credits: page 9 Joan Farre © Dorling Kindersley,
page 15 & 17 Dave King © Dorling Kindersley

ISBN: 978-140930-189-9

Printed in China

A few tips for grown-ups!

The most practical and enjoyable way to learn French with
Max et Mathilde is to listen to the CD and read along, listening
carefully to the pronunciation and then repeating the phrases.

Listen to the CD more than once. Repetition and singing along
will reinforce the vocabulary and phrases in the book.

Let the pictures guide your child. A translation appears at the back of the
book rather than on the page itself to avoid word-for-word translation.

On the right-hand page, the dialogue delivered by Max et Mathilde
is just as French children would speak to each other.

The most important thing is to maintain your child's enthusiasm, motivation
and interest in learning French. Above all, keep it simple and fun!

"Bonjour"

Tu vas apprendre les jours de la semaine.
Tu vas t'amuser!

"Je m'appelle Max."

"Je m'appelle Mathilde."

Le chien
s'appelle Noisette.

lundi

C'est lundi.

Mathilde joue du piano.

mardi

C'est mardi.

Max et Mathilde
vont à la piscine.

"Regarde-moi, Mathilde!
Je nage comme un poisson!"

mercredi

C'est mercredi.

Max et Mathilde
jouent au tennis.

jeudi

C'est jeudi.

Max et Mathilde font
un gâteau au chocolat.

vendredi

C'est vendredi.

Max joue au football
avec son copain.

15

samedi

C'est samedi.

Max et Mathilde
vont pique-niquer.

"Le soleil brille."

"Il fait beau!"

dimanche

C'est dimanche.

Max et Mathilde
restent à la maison.

Translation

"Bonjour!" "Hello!"

Tu vas apprendre les jours de la semaine.
You're going to learn the days of the week.

Tu vas t'amuser! You'll have fun!

"Je m'appelle Max." "My name is Max."

"Je m'appelle Mathilde." "My name is Mathilde."

Les chien s'appelle Noisette. The dog is called Noisette.

lundi Monday

C'est lundi. It's Monday.

Mathilde joue du piano. Mathilde is playing the piano.

"J'aime jouer du piano!" I like playing the piano.

"Je n'aime pas jouer du piano!" I don't like playing the piano.

mardi Tuesday

C'est mardi. It's Tuesday.

Max et Mathilde vont à la piscine.
Max et Mathilde are going to the swimming pool.

"Regarde-moi, Mathilde!" "Look at me, Mathilde!"

"Je nage comme un poisson!" "I can swim like a fish!"

mercredi Wednesday

C'est mercredi. It's Wednesday.

Max et Mathilde jouent au tennis. Max and Mathilde are playing tennis.

"Nous aimons jouer au tennis." "We like playing tennis."

"Je gagne toujours!" "I always win!"

jeudi Thursday

C'est jeudi. It's Thursday.

Max et Mathilde font un gâteau au chocolat.
Max and Mathilde are making a chocolate cake.

"Miam, miam!" "Yum, yum!"

"C'est délicieux!" "It's delicious!"

vendredi Friday

C'est vendredi. It's Friday.

Max joue au football avec son copain. Max is playing football with
his friend.

"Je suis le champion!" "I'm the champion!"

"Non, c'est moi le champion!" "No, I'm the champion!"

samedi Saturday

C'est samedi. It's Saturday.

Max et Mathilde vont pique-niquer.
Max and Mathilde are going on a picnic.

"Le soleil brille." "The sun is shining."

"Il fait beau!" "It's lovely weather!"

dimanche Sunday

C'est dimanche. It's Sunday.

Max et Mathilde restent à la maison.
Max and Mathilde are staying at home.

"Je suis très fatiguée." "I am very tired."

"Moi aussi!" "Me too!"

Now let's play a game!

Can you remember the days of the week?
Find out by answering the questions below.

Quel jour Max et Mathilde vont nager ?

What day do Max and Mathilde go swimming?

Max et Mathilde vont nager le...

Max and Mathilde go swimming on…

Quel jour Max et Mathilde jouent au tennis ?

What day do Max and Mathilde play tennis?

Max et Mathilde jouent au tennis le...

Max and Mathilde play tennis on…

Quel jour Max joue au football ?

What day does Max play football?

Max joue au football le...

Max plays football on…

Quel jour Mathilde joue du piano ?

What day does Mathilde play the piano?

Mathilde joue du piano le...

Mathilde plays piano on...

Quel jour Max et Mathilde restent à la maison ?

What day do Max and Mathilde stay at home?

Max et Mathilde restent à la maison le...

Max et Mathilde stay at home on...

Quel jour Max et Mathilde vont pique-niquer ?

What day do Max et Mathilde go on a picnic?

Max et Mathilde vont pique-niquer le...

Max and Mathilde go on a picnic on...

Now listen to Max et Mathilde on the CD
as they take you through the days of the week.
Chant out loud and sing along with them!

Les jours de la semaine

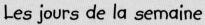

lundi

mardi

mercredi

jeudi

vendredi

samedi

dimanche

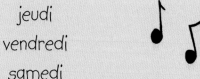

"À bientôt!"